MY DYSFUNCTIONS

KNOCK
KNOCK™
VENICE, CALIFORNIA

Created and published by
Knock Knock
1633 Electric Avenue
Venice, CA 90291
knockknockstuff.com

ISBN: 978-160106074-7
UPC: 825703-50020-2

10 9 8 7 6 5 4 3 2

WE ALL HAVE
ISSUES

We are all self-absorbed. It's all in *our* heads, they're *our* problems, and they're *our* responses to the crazy world we live in. It's natural—our neuroses make us who we are. The idea that anyone has it together, despite the occasional deliberately constructed appearance to the contrary, is a myth. The only thing that separates the men from the boys and the women from the girls is self-awareness. Do you or do you not know that you're half-crazy? Do you celebrate and process your dysfunctions or do you stumble along in blithe denial?

Not only is dysfunction normal and time honored, we live in the era of social pop psychology and antidepressant commercials littered with daisies and sunshine. I'm not okay and you're not okay, and there's a drug for that. Now that we know how to diagnose and name it, 29 percent of the American population has experienced a significant episode of anxiety, and that's merely the reported cases. Approximately 15 percent will suffer from a major depression at some point in their lives. Those who study such things have even ranked countries and states according to their neuroses: Hungary, France, and Switzerland are the most neurotic countries in the world, while West Virginia, Rhode Island, and New York tip the scale among states. In 2008, the American self-help industry—including books, recordings, seminars, and coaching—was $11 billion strong. What are we if not dysfunctional?

While medical professionals first used the term "neurosis" in the mid–nineteenth century, "dysfunction" was not associated with psychology until the 1950s. The rise of the contemporary self-help movement, dating to the late 1970s, cemented our knowledge that we're all abnormal. We have at our disposal a delectable variety of ways to be dysfunctional, from the common to the exotic, including anxiety, depression, phobias, pyromania, post-traumatic stress disorder, and plain old kookiness. Most of us come from dysfunctional families, and we're likely either to repeat our parents' dysfunctions or to manifest new ones as a result of accommodating them.

On the brighter side, dysfunction makes us interesting. The term "tortured artist" had to come from somewhere. Notably brilliant—and neurotic—authors and artists include Salvador Dalí, Charles Dickens, and, of course, Woody Allen. One study found that individuals who'd achieved recognition for their accomplishments exhibited a slightly higher percentage of psychological problems than the general population, with visual artists and writers pulling way ahead of the pack; 75 percent and 90 percent, respectively, contend with mental disturbances. According to Marcel Proust, "Everything great in the world comes from neurotics." Sigmund Freud concluded, "A certain degree of neurosis is of inestimable value as a drive."

We all know that an unexpressed drive is a repressed drive, and repression, indubitably, leads to all manner of problems. Though those of us who are aware of our dysfunctions seek to accept our hang-ups, ultimately we need to keep them in check to live a practical and not entirely miserable existence. Fortunately, the flourishing dysfunction industry means that there are many available tools for those who want to understand, process, and, in some cases, rectify their dysfunctions—and none are more manageable and universally available than the journal.

The benefits of journal writing have been examined, to surprisingly consistent results. According to a widely cited study by James W. Pennebaker and Janel D. Seagal, "Writing about important personal experiences in an emotional way for as little as fifteen minutes over the course of three days brings about improvements in mental and physical health." Proven physical effects include stress management, strengthened immune systems, fewer doctor visits, and improvement in chronic illnesses such as asthma (clearly it's better to vent in your journal than to hyperventilate). "It's hard to believe," says Pennebaker, a psychology professor at the University of Texas at Austin, but "being able to put experiences into words is good for your physical health." Kathleen Adams, founder of the Center for Journal Therapy, calls journals "79-cent therapists."

It's not entirely understood how journaling accomplishes all this. The consensus among experts is that catharsis is involved, but they also point to the organization of experience into a narrative. According to *Newsweek*, some scholars believe that journaling "forces us to transform the ruminations cluttering our minds into coherent stories. Writing about an experience may also dull its emotional impact." Psychologist Ira Progoff, widely considered to be the father of the modern journaling movement, stated in 1975 that an "intensive journal process" could "draw each person's life toward wholeness at its own tempo."

As a devotee of this journal, obviously, you proudly subscribe to both dysfunction's embrace and the transformative powers of journaling. Pink fuzzy covers and gold-plated locks aren't for you—you've chosen a journal that honestly states its purpose. To get the most out of the process, here are a few tips to consider: experts agree that in order to reap the benefits of journaling, you have to stick with it, quasi-daily, for as little as five minutes at a time (at least fifteen minutes, however, is best). Finding regular writing times and comfortable locations can help with consistency. Prompt your writing with questions; in the case of this journal, elaborate on "Why I am dysfunctional today" and "What would make it better." The *My Dysfunctions* journal's quotations will also provide a jumping-off point for your writing. Renowned journaler Anaïs Nin suggests asking yourself, "What feels vivid, warm, or near to you at the moment?" Don't critique your writing as you journal; journaling is a process of self-reflection, not a constructed composition. In other words, spew. Finally, determine a home for your journal where others won't find it.

As someone who recognizes your dysfunctions, you are already ahead of most of the world in self-awareness and insight. Journaling can only help that process—especially in a repository that reflects the true you, neuroses, sarcasm, maladjustment, insanity, and all. Go forth and dysfunction!

Sanity is a cozy lie.

SUSAN SONTAG

WHY I AM DYSFUNCTIONAL TODAY:

_____
_____
_____
_____
_____
_____
_____
_____
_____
_____
_____
_____
_____
_____
_____
_____
_____
_____
_____
_____
_____
_____
_____
_____
_____
_____

WHAT WOULD MAKE IT BETTER TODAY:

I believe that everybody comes from pain and a certain amount of dysfunction.

MARIEL HEMINGWAY

WHY I AM DYSFUNCTIONAL TODAY:

_____

_____

_____

_____

_____

_____

_____

_____

_____

_____

_____

_____

_____

_____

_____

_____

_____

_____

_____

_____

_____

_____

_____

_____

WHAT WOULD MAKE IT BETTER TODAY:

I know I'm paranoid and neurotic; I've made a career out of it.

THOM YORKE

WHY I AM DYSFUNCTIONAL TODAY:

_____
_____
_____
_____
_____
_____
_____
_____
_____
_____
_____
_____
_____
_____
_____
_____
_____
_____
_____
_____
_____
_____
_____
_____
_____
_____
_____

WHAT WOULD MAKE IT BETTER TODAY:

The advantage of the emotions is that they lead us astray.

OSCAR WILDE

DATE		

WHY I AM DYSFUNCTIONAL TODAY:

WHAT WOULD MAKE IT BETTER TODAY:

I found my inner bitch and ran with her.

COURTNEY LOVE

WHY I AM DYSFUNCTIONAL TODAY:

_____

_____

_____

_____

_____

_____

_____

_____

_____

_____

_____

_____

_____

_____

_____

_____

_____

_____

_____

_____

_____

_____

_____

_____

_____

_____

WHAT WOULD MAKE IT BETTER TODAY:

The statistics on sanity are that one out of every four Americans is suffering from some form of mental illness. Think of your three best friends. If they're okay, then it's you.

RITA MAE BROWN

DATE:		

WHY I AM DYSFUNCTIONAL TODAY:

_____

_____

_____

_____

_____

_____

_____

_____

_____

_____

_____

_____

_____

_____

_____

_____

_____

_____

_____

_____

_____

_____

_____

_____

_____

_____

WHAT WOULD MAKE IT BETTER TODAY:

I don't know why
we are here, but
I'm pretty sure that
it is not in order to
enjoy ourselves.

LUDWIG WITTGENSTEIN

DATE		

WHY I AM DYSFUNCTIONAL TODAY:

WHAT WOULD MAKE IT BETTER TODAY:

It's not denial.
I'm just selective
about the reality
I accept.

BILL WATTERSON

WHY I AM DYSFUNCTIONAL TODAY:

_____

_____

_____

_____

_____

_____

_____

_____

_____

_____

_____

_____

_____

_____

_____

_____

_____

_____

_____

_____

_____

_____

_____

_____

_____

WHAT WOULD MAKE IT BETTER TODAY:

A happy childhood is poor preparation for human contacts.

COLETTE

WHY I AM DYSFUNCTIONAL TODAY:

_____
_____
_____
_____
_____
_____
_____
_____
_____
_____
_____
_____
_____
_____
_____
_____
_____
_____
_____
_____
_____
_____
_____
_____

WHAT WOULD MAKE IT BETTER TODAY:

For me, insanity is super sanity. The normal is psychotic. Normal means lack of imagination, lack of creativity.

—————

JEAN DUBUFFET

WHY I AM DYSFUNCTIONAL TODAY:

_____

_____

_____

_____

_____

_____

_____

_____

_____

_____

_____

_____

_____

_____

_____

_____

_____

_____

_____

_____

_____

_____

_____

_____

_____

_____

WHAT WOULD MAKE IT BETTER TODAY:

"Know thyself?"
If I knew myself,
I'd run away.

———————————

JOHANN WOLFGANG VON GOETHE

WHY I AM DYSFUNCTIONAL TODAY:

_____

_____

_____

_____

_____

_____

_____

_____

_____

_____

_____

_____

_____

_____

_____

_____

_____

_____

_____

_____

_____

_____

_____

_____

_____

WHAT WOULD MAKE IT BETTER TODAY:

I prefer neurotic people. I like to hear rumblings beneath the surface.

STEPHEN SONDHEIM

DATE		

WHY I AM DYSFUNCTIONAL TODAY:

_____
_____
_____
_____
_____
_____
_____
_____
_____
_____
_____
_____
_____
_____
_____
_____
_____
_____
_____
_____
_____
_____
_____
_____
_____
_____

WHAT WOULD MAKE IT BETTER TODAY:

When all else fails there's always delusion.

CONAN O'BRIEN

WHY I AM DYSFUNCTIONAL TODAY:

WHAT WOULD MAKE IT BETTER TODAY:

Men can only be
happy when they
do not assume that
the object of life
is happiness.

_____

GEORGE ORWELL

WHY I AM DYSFUNCTIONAL TODAY:

WHAT WOULD MAKE IT BETTER TODAY:

We all live in a house on fire, no fire department to call; no way out, just the upstairs window to look out of while the fire burns the house down with us trapped, locked in it.

—————

TENNESSEE WILLIAMS

DATE		

WHY I AM DYSFUNCTIONAL TODAY:

_____

_____

_____

_____

_____

_____

_____

_____

_____

_____

_____

_____

_____

_____

_____

_____

_____

_____

_____

_____

_____

_____

_____

_____

WHAT WOULD MAKE IT BETTER TODAY:

There is only one
difference between
a madman and me.
I am not mad.

SALVADOR DALÍ

WHY I AM DYSFUNCTIONAL TODAY:

WHAT WOULD MAKE IT BETTER TODAY:

They say best men are molded out of faults, and, for the most, become much more the better for being a little bad.

WILLIAM SHAKESPEARE

DATE		

WHY I AM DYSFUNCTIONAL TODAY:

_____

_____

_____

_____

_____

_____

_____

_____

_____

_____

_____

_____

_____

_____

_____

_____

_____

_____

_____

_____

_____

_____

_____

_____

_____

WHAT WOULD MAKE IT BETTER TODAY:

I cry a lot. My emotions are very close to my surface. I don't want to hold anything in so it festers and turns into pus—a pustule of emotion that explodes into a festering cesspool of depression.

NICOLAS CAGE

DATE		

WHY I AM DYSFUNCTIONAL TODAY:

_____

_____

_____

_____

_____

_____

_____

_____

_____

_____

_____

_____

_____

_____

_____

_____

_____

_____

_____

_____

_____

_____

_____

_____

_____

WHAT WOULD MAKE IT BETTER TODAY:

You're nuts,
but you're
welcome here.

───────────

STEVE MARTIN

WHY I AM DYSFUNCTIONAL TODAY:

_____

_____

_____

_____

_____

_____

_____

_____

_____

_____

_____

_____

_____

_____

_____

_____

_____

_____

_____

_____

_____

_____

_____

WHAT WOULD MAKE IT BETTER TODAY:

If neurotic is wanting two mutually exclusive things at one and the same time, then I'm neurotic as hell. I'll be flying back and forth between one mutually exclusive thing and another for the rest of my days.

SYLVIA PLATH

DATE

WHY I AM DYSFUNCTIONAL TODAY:

_____
_____
_____
_____
_____
_____
_____
_____
_____
_____
_____
_____
_____
_____
_____
_____
_____
_____
_____
_____
_____
_____
_____
_____
_____
_____

WHAT WOULD MAKE IT BETTER TODAY:

I've been the queen of dysfunction and made every mistake one can make.

JANICE DICKINSON

DATE		

WHY I AM DYSFUNCTIONAL TODAY:

_____

_____

_____

_____

_____

_____

_____

_____

_____

_____

_____

_____

_____

_____

_____

_____

_____

_____

_____

_____

_____

_____

_____

_____

_____

_____

_____

_____

_____

WHAT WOULD MAKE IT BETTER TODAY:

All are lunatics, but he who can analyze his delusion is called a philosopher.

AMBROSE BIERCE

DATE		

WHY I AM DYSFUNCTIONAL TODAY:

_____

_____

_____

_____

_____

_____

_____

_____

_____

_____

_____

_____

_____

_____

_____

_____

_____

_____

_____

_____

_____

_____

_____

_____

_____

_____

_____

_____

_____

WHAT WOULD MAKE IT BETTER TODAY:

Sin, guilt, neurosis—
they are one and the
same, the fruit of the
tree of knowledge.

HENRY MILLER

WHY I AM DYSFUNCTIONAL TODAY:

_____
_____
_____
_____
_____
_____
_____
_____
_____
_____
_____
_____
_____
_____
_____
_____
_____
_____
_____
_____
_____
_____
_____
_____

WHAT WOULD MAKE IT BETTER TODAY:

Some people never go crazy. What truly horrible lives they must live.

CHARLES BUKOWSKI

WHY I AM DYSFUNCTIONAL TODAY:

_____

_____

_____

_____

_____

_____

_____

_____

_____

_____

_____

_____

_____

_____

_____

_____

_____

_____

_____

_____

_____

_____

WHAT WOULD MAKE IT BETTER TODAY:

I have cultivated my hysteria with pleasure and terror.

CHARLES BAUDELAIRE

WHY I AM DYSFUNCTIONAL TODAY:

_____
_____
_____
_____
_____
_____
_____
_____
_____
_____
_____
_____
_____
_____
_____
_____
_____
_____
_____
_____
_____
_____
_____
_____
_____
_____

WHAT WOULD MAKE IT BETTER TODAY:

I've been listening to that stupid bastard
I took myself for thirty years ago, hard
to believe I was ever as bad as that.

SAMUEL BECKETT

WHY I AM DYSFUNCTIONAL TODAY:

WHAT WOULD MAKE IT BETTER TODAY:

Oh the nerves, the nerves; the mysteries of this machine called man! Oh the little that unhinges it, poor creatures that we are!

CHARLES DICKENS

WHY I AM DYSFUNCTIONAL TODAY:

_____

_____

_____

_____

_____

_____

_____

_____

_____

_____

_____

_____

_____

_____

_____

_____

_____

_____

_____

_____

_____

_____

_____

WHAT WOULD MAKE IT BETTER TODAY:

I told the doctor
I was overtired,
anxiety ridden,
compulsively active,
constantly depressed,
with recurring fits
of paranoia. Turns
out I'm normal.

JULES FEIFFER

WHY I AM DYSFUNCTIONAL TODAY:

_____

_____

_____

_____

_____

_____

_____

_____

_____

_____

_____

_____

_____

_____

_____

_____

_____

_____

_____

_____

_____

_____

_____

WHAT WOULD MAKE IT BETTER TODAY:

I have a very highly developed sense of denial.

GWYNETH PALTROW

	DATE	

WHY I AM DYSFUNCTIONAL TODAY:

_____

_____

_____

_____

_____

_____

_____

_____

_____

_____

_____

_____

_____

_____

_____

_____

_____

_____

_____

_____

_____

_____

WHAT WOULD MAKE IT BETTER TODAY:

If you can go through life without ever experiencing pain you probably haven't been born yet.

NEIL SIMON

WHY I AM DYSFUNCTIONAL TODAY:

_____

_____

_____

_____

_____

_____

_____

_____

_____

_____

_____

_____

_____

_____

_____

_____

_____

_____

_____

_____

_____

_____

_____

WHAT WOULD MAKE IT BETTER TODAY:

I've always loathed rich people, so
I've become a person who I've loathed.
And I loathed myself even when I wasn't
that person, which makes it doubly
difficult, if you can follow all that.

———————

LARRY DAVID

DATE		

WHY I AM DYSFUNCTIONAL TODAY:

_____

_____

_____

_____

_____

_____

_____

_____

_____

_____

_____

_____

_____

_____

_____

_____

_____

_____

_____

_____

_____

_____

_____

_____

WHAT WOULD MAKE IT BETTER TODAY:

It is much more
comfortable to be
mad and know it
than be sane and
have one's doubts.

G. B. BURGIN

DATE		

WHY I AM DYSFUNCTIONAL TODAY:

_____

_____

_____

_____

_____

_____

_____

_____

_____

_____

_____

_____

_____

_____

_____

_____

_____

_____

_____

_____

_____

_____

_____

_____

_____

_____

WHAT WOULD MAKE IT BETTER TODAY:

Feelings are not supposed to be logical. Dangerous is the man who has rationalized his emotions.

DAVID BORENSTEIN

WHY I AM DYSFUNCTIONAL TODAY:

WHAT WOULD MAKE IT BETTER TODAY:

It's all right letting yourself go, as long as you can get yourself back.

MICK JAGGER

WHY I AM DYSFUNCTIONAL TODAY:

WHAT WOULD MAKE IT BETTER TODAY:

I'm afraid of making a mistake. I'm not totally neurotic, but I'm pretty neurotic about it. I'm as close to totally neurotic as you can get without being totally neurotic.

BRIDGET FONDA

WHY I AM DYSFUNCTIONAL TODAY:

_____

_____

_____

_____

_____

_____

_____

_____

_____

_____

_____

_____

_____

_____

_____

_____

_____

_____

_____

_____

_____

_____

_____

_____

_____

WHAT WOULD MAKE IT BETTER TODAY:

I believe in
looking reality
straight in
the eye and
denying it.

GARRISON KEILLOR

WHY I AM DYSFUNCTIONAL TODAY:

_____

_____

_____

_____

_____

_____

_____

_____

_____

_____

_____

_____

_____

_____

_____

_____

_____

_____

_____

_____

_____

_____

_____

_____

_____

WHAT WOULD MAKE IT BETTER TODAY:

Insane people are always sure they're just fine. It's only the sane people who are willing to admit they're crazy.

NORA EPHRON

DATE		

WHY I AM DYSFUNCTIONAL TODAY:

_____

_____

_____

_____

_____

_____

_____

_____

_____

_____

_____

_____

_____

_____

_____

_____

_____

_____

_____

_____

_____

_____

_____

_____

_____

_____

_____

_____

WHAT WOULD MAKE IT BETTER TODAY:

I can sympathize with people's pains, but not with their pleasures. There is something curiously boring about somebody else's happiness.

ALDOUS HUXLEY

WHY I AM DYSFUNCTIONAL TODAY:

WHAT WOULD MAKE IT BETTER TODAY:

Friends love misery, in fact. Sometimes, especially if we are too lucky or too successful or too pretty, our misery is the only thing that endears us to our friends.

ERICA JONG

WHY I AM DYSFUNCTIONAL TODAY:

_____
_____
_____
_____
_____
_____
_____
_____
_____
_____
_____
_____
_____
_____
_____
_____
_____
_____
_____
_____
_____
_____
_____
_____

WHAT WOULD MAKE IT BETTER TODAY:

He who despises himself
nevertheless esteems
himself as a self-despiser.

FRIEDRICH NIETZSCHE

WHY I AM DYSFUNCTIONAL TODAY:

_____
_____
_____
_____
_____
_____
_____
_____
_____
_____
_____
_____
_____
_____
_____
_____
_____
_____
_____
_____
_____
_____
_____
_____
_____
_____
_____
_____
_____

WHAT WOULD MAKE IT BETTER TODAY:

If we cannot be happy and powerful and prey on others, we invent conscience and prey on ourselves.

ELBERT HUBBARD

WHY I AM DYSFUNCTIONAL TODAY:

_____
_____
_____
_____
_____
_____
_____
_____
_____
_____
_____
_____
_____
_____
_____
_____
_____
_____
_____
_____
_____
_____
_____
_____

WHAT WOULD MAKE IT BETTER TODAY:

I know whenever
it comes to be
really dysfunctional
and vile and base
and hostile on
screen, I'm good
at that!

WERNER HERZOG

WHY I AM DYSFUNCTIONAL TODAY:

_____

_____

_____

_____

_____

_____

_____

_____

_____

_____

_____

_____

_____

_____

_____

_____

_____

_____

_____

_____

_____

_____

_____

WHAT WOULD MAKE IT BETTER TODAY:

It is sometimes
an appropriate
response to reality
to go insane.

PHILIP K. DICK

DATE		

WHY I AM DYSFUNCTIONAL TODAY:

_____

_____

_____

_____

_____

_____

_____

_____

_____

_____

_____

_____

_____

_____

_____

_____

_____

_____

_____

_____

_____

_____

_____

_____

WHAT WOULD MAKE IT BETTER TODAY:

Everything great in the world comes from neurotics. They alone have founded our religions and composed our masterpieces.

MARCEL PROUST

DATE		

WHY I AM DYSFUNCTIONAL TODAY:

_____

_____

_____

_____

_____

_____

_____

_____

_____

_____

_____

_____

_____

_____

_____

_____

_____

_____

_____

_____

_____

WHAT WOULD MAKE IT BETTER TODAY:

It's crazy how you can get yourself in
a mess sometimes and not even be able
to think about it with any sense and yet
not be able to think about anything else.

STANLEY KUBRICK

DATE		

WHY I AM DYSFUNCTIONAL TODAY:

WHAT WOULD MAKE IT BETTER TODAY:

Delusions of grandeur make me feel a lot better about myself.

LILY TOMLIN

WHY I AM DYSFUNCTIONAL TODAY:

_____

_____

_____

_____

_____

_____

_____

_____

_____

_____

_____

_____

_____

_____

_____

_____

_____

_____

_____

_____

_____

_____

_____

_____

WHAT WOULD MAKE IT BETTER TODAY:

A life based on reason will always require to be balanced by an occasional bout of violent and irrational emotion, for the instinctual drives must be satisfied.

CYRIL CONNOLLY

WHY I AM DYSFUNCTIONAL TODAY:

_____
_____
_____
_____
_____
_____
_____
_____
_____
_____
_____
_____
_____
_____
_____
_____
_____
_____
_____
_____
_____
_____
_____
_____

WHAT WOULD MAKE IT BETTER TODAY:

I always say
shopping
is cheaper
than a
psychiatrist.

TAMMY FAYE BAKKER

DATE		

WHY I AM DYSFUNCTIONAL TODAY:

_____

_____

_____

_____

_____

_____

_____

_____

_____

_____

_____

_____

_____

_____

_____

_____

_____

_____

_____

_____

_____

_____

_____

_____

_____

_____

WHAT WOULD MAKE IT BETTER TODAY:

If my devils are to leave me, I am afraid my angels will take flight as well.

RAINER MARIA RILKE

WHY I AM DYSFUNCTIONAL TODAY:

WHAT WOULD MAKE IT BETTER TODAY:

You may be right

I may be crazy

But it just may be a lunatic
   you're looking for.

BILLY JOEL

WHY I AM DYSFUNCTIONAL TODAY:

_____

_____

_____

_____

_____

_____

_____

_____

_____

_____

_____

_____

_____

_____

_____

_____

_____

_____

_____

_____

_____

_____

_____

_____

_____

_____

WHAT WOULD MAKE IT BETTER TODAY:

Denial ain't just a river in Egypt.

MARK TWAIN

DATE		

WHY I AM DYSFUNCTIONAL TODAY:

_____

_____

_____

_____

_____

_____

_____

_____

_____

_____

_____

_____

_____

_____

_____

_____

_____

_____

_____

_____

_____

_____

_____

_____

_____

WHAT WOULD MAKE IT BETTER TODAY:

A certain degree of neurosis is of inestimable value as a drive, especially to a psychologist.

SIGMUND FREUD

DATE		

WHY I AM DYSFUNCTIONAL TODAY:

WHAT WOULD MAKE IT BETTER TODAY:

See, the human mind is kind of like . . .
a piñata. When it breaks open, there's a
lot of surprises inside. Once you get the
piñata perspective, you see that losing
your mind can be a peak experience.

JANE WAGNER

WHY I AM DYSFUNCTIONAL TODAY:

_____

_____

_____

_____

_____

_____

_____

_____

_____

_____

_____

_____

_____

_____

_____

_____

_____

_____

_____

_____

_____

_____

_____

WHAT WOULD MAKE IT BETTER TODAY:

I wouldn't recommend sex, drugs, or insanity for everyone, but they've always worked for me.

HUNTER S. THOMPSON

WHY I AM DYSFUNCTIONAL TODAY:

_____

_____

_____

_____

_____

_____

_____

_____

_____

_____

_____

_____

_____

_____

_____

_____

_____

_____

_____

_____

_____

_____

_____

_____

_____

WHAT WOULD MAKE IT BETTER TODAY:

Perhaps the only true dignity of man is his capacity to despise himself.

GEORGE SANTAYANA

DATE		

WHY I AM DYSFUNCTIONAL TODAY:

WHAT WOULD MAKE IT BETTER TODAY:

All successful people these days seem to be neurotic. Perhaps we should stop being sorry for them and start being sorry for me—for being so confounded normal.

DEBORAH KERR

WHY I AM DYSFUNCTIONAL TODAY:

WHAT WOULD MAKE IT BETTER TODAY:

There is no great genius without tincture of madness.

SENECA

DATE:		

WHY I AM DYSFUNCTIONAL TODAY:

_____

_____

_____

_____

_____

_____

_____

_____

_____

_____

_____

_____

_____

_____

_____

_____

_____

_____

_____

_____

_____

_____

_____

_____

_____

_____

WHAT WOULD MAKE IT BETTER TODAY:

I exist in a state
of almost perpetual
hysteria.

STING

DATE		

WHY I AM DYSFUNCTIONAL TODAY:

_____

_____

_____

_____

_____

_____

_____

_____

_____

_____

_____

_____

_____

_____

_____

_____

_____

_____

_____

_____

_____

_____

_____

WHAT WOULD MAKE IT BETTER TODAY:

The good die young—because they see
it's no use living if you've got to be good.

JOHN BARRYMORE

DATE		

WHY I AM DYSFUNCTIONAL TODAY:

_____

_____

_____

_____

_____

_____

_____

_____

_____

_____

_____

_____

_____

_____

_____

_____

_____

_____

_____

_____

_____

_____

_____

_____

_____

_____

_____

_____

_____

_____

WHAT WOULD MAKE IT BETTER TODAY:

I was the captain of the latent paranoid softball team. We used to play all the neurotics on Sunday morning. The nail biters against the bed wetters. But if you've never seen neurotics play softball, it's really funny. I used to steal second base, then feel guilty and go back.

———

WOODY ALLEN

DATE		

WHY I AM DYSFUNCTIONAL TODAY:

_____

_____

_____

_____

_____

_____

_____

_____

_____

_____

_____

_____

_____

_____

_____

_____

_____

_____

_____

_____

_____

_____

_____

_____

_____

_____

_____

_____

_____

_____

WHAT WOULD MAKE IT BETTER TODAY:

In a well-run mental household there ought to be a thorough cleaning at the threshold of consciousness a few times a year.

KARL KRAUS

	DATE	

WHY I AM DYSFUNCTIONAL TODAY:

_____

_____

_____

_____

_____

_____

_____

_____

_____

_____

_____

_____

_____

_____

_____

_____

_____

_____

_____

_____

_____

_____

_____

WHAT WOULD MAKE IT BETTER TODAY:

There's a fine line between genius and insanity. I have erased this line.

OSCAR LEVANT

WHY I AM DYSFUNCTIONAL TODAY:

WHAT WOULD MAKE IT BETTER TODAY:

I'm a neurotic—in the sense that I live in *my* world. I will not adjust myself to *the* world. I am adjusted to myself.

———

ANAÏS NIN

WHY I AM DYSFUNCTIONAL TODAY:

_____

_____

_____

_____

_____

_____

_____

_____

_____

_____

_____

_____

_____

_____

_____

_____

_____

_____

_____

_____

_____

_____

_____

_____

WHAT WOULD MAKE IT BETTER TODAY:

Doubt is not a pleasant condition,
but certainty is an absurd one.

———

VOLTAIRE

DATE		

WHY I AM DYSFUNCTIONAL TODAY:

_____
_____
_____
_____
_____
_____
_____
_____
_____
_____
_____
_____
_____
_____
_____
_____
_____
_____
_____
_____
_____
_____
_____
_____
_____

WHAT WOULD MAKE IT BETTER TODAY:

Happiness is having a large, loving, caring, close-knit family in another city.

GEORGE BURNS

DATE		

WHY I AM DYSFUNCTIONAL TODAY:

_____

_____

_____

_____

_____

_____

_____

_____

_____

_____

_____

_____

_____

_____

_____

_____

_____

_____

_____

_____

_____

_____

_____

_____

_____

WHAT WOULD MAKE IT BETTER TODAY:

You're only given a little spark
of madness. You mustn't lose it.

ROBIN WILLIAMS

DATE	

WHY I AM DYSFUNCTIONAL TODAY:

_____

_____

_____

_____

_____

_____

_____

_____

_____

_____

_____

_____

_____

_____

_____

_____

_____

_____

_____

_____

_____

_____

WHAT WOULD MAKE IT BETTER TODAY:

There is a luxury
in self-reproach.
When we blame
ourselves we feel
no one else has a
right to blame us.

OSCAR WILDE

WHY I AM DYSFUNCTIONAL TODAY:

_____

_____

_____

_____

_____

_____

_____

_____

_____

_____

_____

_____

_____

_____

_____

_____

_____

_____

_____

_____

_____

_____

_____

_____

_____

_____

_____

_____

_____

_____

_____

WHAT WOULD MAKE IT BETTER TODAY:

If you commit a big crime then you are crazy, and the more heinous the crime the crazier you must be. Therefore you are not responsible, and nothing is your fault.

PEGGY NOONAN

WHY I AM DYSFUNCTIONAL TODAY:

_____

_____

_____

_____

_____

_____

_____

_____

_____

_____

_____

_____

_____

_____

_____

_____

_____

_____

_____

_____

_____

_____

_____

WHAT WOULD MAKE IT BETTER TODAY:

The final delusion
is the belief that one
has lost all delusions.

MAURICE CHAPELAIN

DATE		

WHY I AM DYSFUNCTIONAL TODAY:

_____

_____

_____

_____

_____

_____

_____

_____

_____

_____

_____

_____

_____

_____

_____

_____

_____

_____

_____

_____

_____

_____

WHAT WOULD MAKE IT BETTER TODAY:

Hope—in reality
it is the worst
of all evils, because
it prolongs the
torments of man.

_____

FRIEDRICH NIETZSCHE

DATE		

WHY I AM DYSFUNCTIONAL TODAY:

_____
_____
_____
_____
_____
_____
_____
_____
_____
_____
_____
_____
_____
_____
_____
_____
_____
_____
_____
_____
_____
_____
_____
_____
_____
_____
_____

WHAT WOULD MAKE IT BETTER TODAY:

When we remember that we are all
mad, the mysteries disappear and
life stands explained.

MARK TWAIN

WHY I AM DYSFUNCTIONAL TODAY:

_____

_____

_____

_____

_____

_____

_____

_____

_____

_____

_____

_____

_____

_____

_____

_____

_____

_____

_____

_____

_____

_____

_____

_____

_____

_____

_____

WHAT WOULD MAKE IT BETTER TODAY:

To be too conscious is an illness—
a real thoroughgoing illness.

——————

FYODOR DOSTOEVSKY

WHY I AM DYSFUNCTIONAL TODAY:

WHAT WOULD MAKE IT BETTER TODAY:

I became insane,
with long intervals
of horrible sanity.

EDGAR ALLAN POE

	DATE	

WHY I AM DYSFUNCTIONAL TODAY:

_____

_____

_____

_____

_____

_____

_____

_____

_____

_____

_____

_____

_____

_____

_____

_____

_____

_____

_____

_____

_____

_____

_____

_____

_____

_____

WHAT WOULD MAKE IT BETTER TODAY:

Self-pity—it's the only
pity that counts.

OSCAR LEVANT

DATE	

WHY I AM DYSFUNCTIONAL TODAY:

_____

_____

_____

_____

_____

_____

_____

_____

_____

_____

_____

_____

_____

_____

_____

_____

_____

_____

_____

_____

_____

_____

_____

_____

_____

_____

_____

_____

_____

WHAT WOULD MAKE IT BETTER TODAY:

The average,
healthy, well-
adjusted adult
gets up at
seven-thirty
in the morning
feeling just
plain terrible.

JEAN KERR

DATE	

WHY I AM DYSFUNCTIONAL TODAY:

_____

_____

_____

_____

_____

_____

_____

_____

_____

_____

_____

_____

_____

_____

_____

_____

_____

_____

_____

_____

_____

_____

_____

_____

_____

_____

_____

_____

_____

_____

WHAT WOULD MAKE IT BETTER TODAY:

All men should strive to learn
    before they die

what they are running from,
    and to, and why.

——————

JAMES THURBER

DATE		

WHY I AM DYSFUNCTIONAL TODAY:

_____

_____

_____

_____

_____

_____

_____

_____

_____

_____

_____

_____

_____

_____

_____

_____

_____

_____

_____

_____

_____

_____

_____

_____

_____

_____

_____

_____

_____

_____

WHAT WOULD MAKE IT BETTER TODAY:

We're more interesting if we are dysfunctional.

RUPERT EVERETT

DATE	

WHY I AM DYSFUNCTIONAL TODAY:

_____
_____
_____
_____
_____
_____
_____
_____
_____
_____
_____
_____
_____
_____
_____
_____
_____
_____
_____
_____
_____
_____
_____

WHAT WOULD MAKE IT BETTER TODAY:

It's not my fault.

_____

KNOCK KNOCK